PRECOCIOUS
ADAM LOWE

Published by Fruit Bruise Press
an imprint of
Dog Horn Publishing
45 Monk Ings
Birstall
Batley
WF17 9HU
doghornpublishing.com

About the Author

Adam Lowe is a writer and publisher from Leeds. He has been nominated for four Lambda Literary Awards, three British Fantasy Awards and the Eric Hoffer Award. In 2008, his magazine, *Polluto*, was awarded a Spectrum Fantastic Art Award. He has held a number of residencies, including I Love West Leeds Festival, Zion Arts Centre and West Yorkshire Playhouse. He has had commissions from and collaborated with the BBC, Channel 4, Endemol, Olympics 2012, imove, Manchester Pride, Manchester Tourism Board, Leeds Racial Harassment Project, Light Night, International Seas Festival and Leeds Lieder+.

Adam is a graduate of Street Voices and continues to be an active member of Young Inscribe. Adam regularly delivers workshops and runs an annual writer development programme for new writers in the North: the Dog Horn Masterclasses. Because of his work in the region, he is a Youth Ambassador for the Cultural Olympiad.

He has appeared in *Word Riot, Unlikely Stories, Cadaverine, Chimeraworld 5, Leeds Guide, WAMACK, Saucytooth's, Kaleidotrope, PoetCasting*, and *Ex Plus Ultra*. He has work forthcoming in *Cake* and *SABLE LitMag*, with his second novella due out from Dead Ink Press in 2012. Adam's academic writing has appeared at University of Glasgow's *eSharp* and is forthcoming in *Queering the Fantastic*. His debut novella, *Troglodyte Rose*, was released in limited hardback by Cadaverine Publications. An expanded novel-length version is currently with a major publisher.

The poem/play 'Friend Roulette', included in this collection, was produced and performed at the Royal Exchange Theatre in July 2011. His BBC-commissioned short play 'Deep Blue Skin' was showcased in March 2011 at West Yorkshire Playhouse. Plays have also been produced at Zion Arts Centre, Theatre in the Mill, Stage @ Leeds, outside the DSS building in Leeds, and Arts @ Trinity. He is currently working on his next novel.

ADAM-LOWE.COM

FRIEND ROULETTE

Two figutres sat in darkness. Laptops open. The darkness between them, a worldwide web.

Mod: Welcome to FriendRoulette. Log in or register?
A: Log in.
Mod: Would you like FriendRoulette to remember these log in details?
A: Yes.
Mod: You are home. You have ONE new message. You have had 23 profile hits this week.
A: Messages.
B: Hey, what's your pleasure?
A: My pleasure?
B: What you looking for? What's your poison, dude?
A: Looking for chat, fun, mates. Etc.
B: Okay.
A: You?
B: Etc.

Blackout.

Mod: Welcome back to FriendRoulette. Log in or register?
A: Log in.
Mod: Log in details remembered. You are home.
A: One new message.
B: Are you there?
A: Yeah. Just got in.
B: Me too.
A: How was your day?
B: Tiring.
A: Yeah?
B: Been shopping with my sister. You?
A: Been at uni.
B: What are you studying?
A: Sociology.
B: Smart.
A: Not really LOL.
B: Well we can pretend ;)

Blackout.

Mod: Welcome back to FriendRoulette. Log in or register?
A: Log in.
Mod: Log in details remembered. You are home.
A: Where are we?
B: We're at the cathedral. Sunlight spools from above.

3

A: Tell me.

B: I'm telling you. You're on the grass. Skinny jeans. I'm sitting opposite you, licking a rolly sealed.

A: I can taste the glue on your tongue. Can feel your lips kiss the silky skin closed.

B: You're good at this.

A: I suddenly feel creative.

B: Why?

A: I don't know.

B: Come here.

A: Where are you?

Blackout.

Mod: Welcome back to FriendRoulette. You are home.

B: I'm here. Your lips are on me.

A: My tongue slides into your mouth.

B: Your body softens against me even as you harden.

A: I'm so hard.

B: Like a bulb against my leg.

A: Pressing tight against you.

B: I want to fold into you.

A: Unfold me.

B: Light me up.

Blackout.

B: I unfold you. I speak into the blank, open book of you. Breathe words across your pages. You are starting to take shape: listing lines of black. Forming a story. I reach out. I poke you.

B: This is my space. Take a look at me.

B: Come inside, I say. Come inside me.

Blackout.

Mod: Welcome back to FriendRoulette. Log in or register?

A: Log in.

Mod: Log in details remembered. You are home.

A: A home I can feel through
in the dark, moving between walls
unnoticed, master of its geometries
as they slumber, unmapped, undrawn.

Mod: Welcome back to FriendRoulette. Log in or register?

B: Log in.

Mod: Log in details remembered. You are home.

B: A home I can fill, a warm
pool of myself, contained
shapely, ready to flow under
doorways, along skirting.

Mod: Welcome back to FriendRoulette. Log in or register?
A: Log in.
Mod: Log in details remembered. You are home.

A: A home I can dream around
me: a welcome artistry, shaped
to the contours of my soft
mathematics, centred, encircled, whole.

Blackout.

Mod: Welcome back to FriendRoulette. Log in or register?
A: Log in.
Mod: Log in details remembered. You are home.
B: We are alone here. This is a world we have created. The forest at our
back is a velvet emerald burst open. The azaleas are crimson-pink, open
chalices brimming with ambrosia. You pick one from its slim stalk, raise
the cup to your mouth, and drink of the champagne nectar.

A: In the garden you burrow into my soil, and plant yourself in the bed
of me.

Blackout.

Mod: Welcome back to FriendRoulette. Log in or register?
B: Log in.
Mod: Log in details remembered. You are home.
A: What if we met?
B: What?
A: What if it went wrong?
B: It might. That's half the fun.
A: It might go very wrong.
B: It might.

Blackout.

B: You wait by the frozen turkeys,
covered in goosebumps. Through your
joggers I can see your icicle dick,
the shape of it. Long. I've got
my hand on frozen peas, an excuse

to be here at 3am. Just the noise
of shelf-stackers in the crisps aisle,
enough to cover the rustle as you slide
your hand down, revealing a bulge
in white Ginch Gonch. You pop it
out, creamy as a Mini Milk, and stroke
it gently, working forefinger and thumb
towards the tip. I don't move
but I watch, as you spill spunk
all over the cryo-sleep poultry.

B: I buy the peas, some milk,
and a Calippo, and checking
my palm, I feel short-changed.

Blackout.

A: I need to go.
B: What?
A: I need to get out.
B: Why?
A: I've been sat in this darkness for days with you. I'm spinning in
darkness.
B: What?
A: I need to see what's outside.
B: You know what's outside. It's the same as it's always been. It's only in
here that things can change.
A: I'm stuck in FriendRoulette waiting for the loaded chamber.
B: Pardon?
A: The bullet in the gun.
B: Yes, the bullet's in the gun.
A: No. I need to see what's out there. To see if it really exists any more.
B: But isn't this perfect here?
A: It is but . . .
B: What?
A: It's not real.
B: It's real enough. Virtually.
A: I'm not so sure.
B: It was enough for you before.
A: Yes.
B: Will the outside be enough?
A: I'm not sure. Maybe I need both?
B: So you'll come back?
A: Maybe.
B: Maybe?
A: Tomorrow, we might both be somebody new.

Blackout.

A: This is the way out. I can see it up ahead. Bright.
Sunlight. People move past me without usernames.
We are not friends. They stand in profile, their secrets their own.
They pass me. I have logged out but I am switched on.

Mod: You are now logged out of FriendRoulette. Log in as somebody
else or exit?
A: Exit.
Mod: Remain logged in next time?
A: No.
Mod: Preferences remembered. You are logged out. You are home.

Blackout.

A: What's your pleasure?
B: Fun.
A: What's your poison?
B: I want to taste you.
A: I'll be your poison. I'll let you drink from me.
B: Bet you taste sweet.
A: I do. Come taste what rivers here.
B: It's wet.
A: It's warm.
B: It is warm.
A: Can you smell it?
B: Yes.
A: Smells like flowers.
B: Smells like nectar.
A: Smells like poison.
B: Smells real.
A: Come. Drink deep.
B: Tasty.
A: Swirl in me. Come in me.

THE OFFER

after Grace Nichols

Fag boy declines
your offer
to take part
in society

instead he turns
his back on
        government
        police and
        money

he'll sit at home
write a poem
roll over in
his bed

he'll hike up hills
and sleep in caves
knead and bake
his own bread

fag boy sees
the snares you lay
the world with which
you trap

        he wants to write
        he wants to sing
        he wants to kick back

BONE RAILROAD

I will clutch your bones together
into a coral palace at the bottom
of the sea. I will sing hymns

to celebrate you in the vault
built from your ribcage. The stained
glass I will blow from your dreams.

Who cast you down here like
a bone railroad from Africa's west
coast to the Americas, the Caribbean?

Whales will worship you.
I will come down and sit upon
your coral throne, and remember

who you were. I will unearth
your stories, find the ships that
discarded you, and sink them all.

AFTERLIFE @ AFTERSHOCK

Pass the dry-ice strobe-stare of the
three-headed bouncer there, pass
the hellhound with six black shoulders.
Descend with me into a bruise-lit underworld.
Anna Phylactic, our Queen Ishtar, rules
with eye-patch, hoop-skirt, wig.
Cyclopean giver of asphodel foams
at his grinning mouth, collects payment from
all to lift them, high spirits, to heaven;
and the DJ, hand cutting tunes like
a scythe, ferries us to the shore of the next
blue dawn. Bass rumbles, the displeasure
of life against ecstasy; then the drop comes
and we're wing-swept to rapture as one.

TRACES OF INVASION

I start with your sock drawer,
looking for clues. He's not in the bathroom
where the usual signs should be found:
toothbrush, aftershave, maybe a razor
or spare inhaler. Neither is he in your
kitchen, a metaphor in spoons or knives,
rustling when one of us hungers. Nor
is he in the lounge, in the favourite pre-set
TV channels, the choice of furniture, or
the lived-in smell of your home.

So he must be in your bedroom,
hiding from one day to the next
between the mattress and bed, or
under your wardrobe. But he's left
none of his clothes: tidy, unlike me,
who leaves traces of invasion like pus
dotted wherever I've been. Does he know?
Does he see me in the water streaks
of your mirror, or smell me in the carpet
when you fuck him bareback on the floor
where you like to fuck me? I find him
eventually, misplaced among towels,
where a polaroid falls like it was buried
treasure, pressed between His and His.

MARY

Forget stars, spoiling the night
with septic limelight. This time
I'll rely on a real man—not some
gynaephobe who sends a sterile
angel in scrubs, carrying a turkey baster
to impress me with His seed. I only
knew Him as dove white Spirit brought
like a shooter in a divine vessel. Next time
I want out of the public eye. Let my child
be down-to-earth, not sent sky-high. Give her
kisses not thorns and nails. If He tries
filling me with promises and lies, or
any more of His Holy Kids, I'll remind him
it's my choice. I'll tell him it really is
bad form to knock me up and ruin
my figure, without first even buying
me dinner. At least Zeus showered
girls with gold, and gave them sons
to hold planets on their shoulders. No,
not again. I'll be no Lord's Madonna.

TRYST WITH THE DEVIL

Come. Let me show you dewy wonders
here in the grass. Let me feel the flicker
of your tongue in my arse. Come

slide over me, muscular river,
rockstar-pornstar in the shape of an asp.
Splash your coat of stars across me,

wrap me in your night. Prophet
of rebels, wet me with your meteorites.
With tongue I'll trace your proud descent.

King of things that scrabble in the dirt,
let me know your defiance. Let me raise
your fallen army—I'll command it.

FEAR

When our bodies knuckled
and slithered against each other,
all I could taste was your blood
seeping through your pores
as it poured into me. Your ink
was a swirling nebula, my skin
exploded, the strings of your
heart knotting through mine.
Intertwined, trapped, we spooled,
gnawed, fed. I worried myself
sick of your sick, felt it rise
as fire and tar through my quick.
We released, later, shaking,
ribbons of stitching undone.

SEEDER

Welcome to the Pirate Bay,
where cruiser comes to dock,
towing net through torrents

of virtual saltwater. Raw data
streams to your harddrive: a virus,
ghost in the machine, blossoms

into electric bundles, cascades style
on the sheets, shares contraband seed.
Information, like disease, desires to be free.

FALLOUT

We lived in a constant winter, nuclear
families bathed daily in silver-blue
Narnian snow. We drew hopscotch
grids in a silted school playground
and tasted dusty fingers, like it was
sherbet or fairy dust, consuming
hourglass sands to percolate in pink,
young lungs. We balled fistfuls, spat
to make sticky dough patties, then
hurled them, slow-acting fast bombs,
at siblings, friends, stray dogs. Dust
clouds rested in situ, slowly breathed
sparkling rain down on streets where
the asbestos was as thick as cotton.
We lived thereafter in the fallout.

DENYING MY PASSION
IN THE MOONLIGHT

Limned by grace of light,
the candle embellishes you.
Gone, in the umbrage of the study:
the rabbets of your sunken chest,
the crimp of turkey dulap,
the trenches of your shoulders
and the flutes of your spine
rolling between them like a bodice.

The shadow hides your waste,
as the glow flourishes the strips
of skin still pink.

Your white nightshirt yaws
seraphic in the candle's nimbus,
and I forget the scalloped stomach,
the desiccated limbs at your side,
as you rot inside out from
knotted nodules, bubbling
festoons on velutinous organs.

I can pretend with fervour
your body is a sacred chalice,
that I sip when we kiss;
and when the dawn falls in,
revealing the scoops and shallows
of your tenuous form, gently,
I pretend not to fear.

TRACY EMIN

after David Tait

I lie in state above our covers and hit your voicemail.
I want to talk about Tracy Emin as I read the sheets.

I imagine we're riding her bed. Its a sordid flying
carpet dragged down the effluent of the Thames.

We leave a greasy smear on the surface,
and sail through clouds of purple smoke.

I'm mortified, unable to enjoy London Bridge,
its iron speckled with dried blood orange.

I'm glad for the beep and the silence
that follows. I haven't paid your bill.

I'll imagine I'm the cigarettes, you're the ash.
I'll lie a while longer. This call can wait.

HER HEART

The queen wanted her heart, saw in the mirror the beauty
of her and saw she must have it, that she must have her heart.

She felt cold for the want of that white skin, like snow, she longed
to be wrapped in. She felt black inside, an evil ebony, for the desire

to put that hair in her mouth. She bled jealousy for the colour
of those lips; felt constricted by that tiny waist, those wide

woman's hips; wanted to bind her, comb bone teeth through her hair—
but mostly, when she looked in the mirror, the queen wanted her heart.

SNOW WHITE
IN THE GRAVEYARD

after Jackie Kay

At night the blooms in your flesh
clench like fists in the graveyard where
you sleep beneath pebble-dashed stars.

Mahler haunts in stink from organs
the worms play from dusk to twilight.
You are slow as glaciers, skin

turned translucent in the gaze
of the moon. Your sleep mutates
the shape of the silence, marble cold

without lyrics. Your presence turns to mist.
Once I kissed you to see if you'd awaken
but . . . I guess I'm no prince.

ICE ANGEL

And he reached for the stars,
ambitious despite the creeping
tendrils of frost. He longed to touch
the moon, a full pendant of ice bulbous
against indigo marble in the sky; thought
in the rapture he could work miracles,
walk on water, drunk on the sublime.
He wanted to cross over and lift on shifts
of starlight. Instead the crisp surface cracked,
as his first foot descended, sank, clasped by
still waters. Then the second foot too, until
he was captured in waxy tableau. Trapped,
he's there still: an ice angel poised
beneath impenetrable glass.

VADA THAT

after Lady Mary Wroth

Aunt nell the patterflash and gardy loo!
Bijou, she trolls, bold on lallies slick as stripes
down the Dilly. She minces past the brandy latch

to vada dolly dish for trade, silly with oomph
and taste to park. She'll reef you on your vagaries—
should you be so lucky. She plans to gam a steamer

and tip the brandy, but give her starters
and she'll be happy to give up for the harva.
Mais oui, she's got your number, duckie.

She'll cruise an omi with fabulosa bod,
regard the scotches, the thews, the rod—
charpering a carsey for the trick.

Slick, she bamboozles the ogles of old Lilly Law.
She swishes through town, 'alf meshigener,
and blows lamors through the oxy at all

the passing trade. She'll sass a drink of aqua da vida,
wallop with vera in claw. Nellyarda her voche's chant
till the nochy with panache becomes journo,

till the sparkle laus the munge out of guard.
Though she's got nada, she aches for an affaire,
and dreams of pogey through years of nix.

The game nanti works —not for her. She prefers a head
or back slum to the meat rack. She'll end up in
the fist of Jennifer Justice. What is this queer ken

she's in? Give her an auntie or a mama. The bones
isn't needed just yet. She's a bimbo bit of hard, royal
and tart. But girl, vadaing her eek is always bona.

THE KISS

We kiss in front of your monument,
our lips pressed like this, the ovals
of mouths bunched into fists.

We hold tight with soft arms,
and tango in rows, our bodies
all faces and hooked elbows.

We kiss outside parliament
to show you we're here. We kiss
in the street. We kiss without fear.

CHIP WRAP COLLÁGE

We commit seppuku
with a broken pint glass,
there in the chip wrap
collage of the gutter.

Amongst half-eaten kebabs,
we pray for the focus
of the lamppost spotlight
to make us worthwhile.

Your blood and mine
seeps together. Laughing
kids come and piss on us
in our tarmac deathbed.

We hang on for the pokes
of strangers, the fame of a
YouTube death rattle. Violet
in the half-light, we slowly

fade to black. It's when
the crowd disappears
and the filming stops that
we know it's finally over.

ROADRAGE

for Frida Kahlo

Metal tangled through me, razor fingers
driven in, a cold handshake—a fist.

A red sea opened in the soil beneath
my shattered hip. Stars broke out of me,

dazzled eyes with fool's gold. My nerves
became barbed wire. The teeth of the road

burrowed inside, melded in heat
to my bones. After I was picked

from the wreckage I healed,
but the road's rage inside me grows.

DEVOTION

I never believed in devotion till
it started to grow, the change claiming me
too: round crocodile belly, harbouring
something it shouldn't. So we began in
fits to make of the house an ark, aware
God must wish to wash this creature away
in waves. I grew a tail, great for steering
when we could finally sail the ocean.

I knew it was dark, swirling at my root,
grinding teeth as my own grew sharper too.
Soon I would be ready, so it could come
slide free from my flesh and begin to feed.

As the rain fell I learned the grand plan:
to fill itself on the fat of the land.

A REVENGE IN SCARLET

Female genital mutilation (FGM) comprises all procedures that involve
partial or total removal of the external female genitalia, or other injury to
the female genital organs for non-medical reasons.
—World Health Organisation website (who.int)

I am dervish-winds howling through
your rose garden, ragging myself open
on thorns. Envious of cleft things, spreading
petals. I take to the flowers we planted
with secateurs, leave them decapitated, Anne Boleyne.

Mute, dead brides, all. Daughters too. Because
I am silenced, stitched up. My lips sewn
to a pleasing rictus grin. Light cannot reach
the bulbs and tubers scrolled apocryphal inside.
I am fallow. And you who grew me pruned me.

So in revenge, I butcher with a flourish your garden
in scarlet; seal it with salt and lime. Nothing shall bloom
with my rage a blossoming stain. Lying by the wall,
I take parrot-beak shears, cut myself open again.

KIND

This is no kind of a life: stations,
waiting, clutching newspapers
so fiercely the type imprints itself
as hexes on my skin.

This is no kind of a life: my love
a takeaway you order to your door
when alone, forbidden, dirty as your dishes,
still no main course. Separated,

this is no kind of a life; divided
by secrecy and mountains; unheard
because I know you won't answer
your telephone. No,

this is no kind of a life,
between lives, praying through
the rain on your doorstep
for you to let me in.

This is no kind of a life, lived
in doorways and corridors,
stolen between moments,
a life I won't live any more.

CORPSE

Now this cool mould of flesh
tells stories about me. It reveals
a taste for the finer things: deep
glasses of red wine, fine cuts of meat,
buttery asparagus spears in my side.

It tells lies of my morality, discloses
the scars of smoke and powders snuffed.
It says nothing of a passion for poetry,
unless I've missed the papercuts.

It hides those loves that ringed my heart—
whether jovial or saturnine. It keeps
the glisten of surprise in the eye (now hooded).
Its drive, become suppurated muscle, is gone.
This eulogy must be enough.

THE LAST STRING OF RAINBOW IS LAVENDER

after Rommi Smith

You wore distance then.
You were an atlas to be circled
for water and treasure.

I knew all the lies and all the stories.
I'd had so much knowledge
I'd grown sore.

But a strange land lends
new innocence. So naive once more,
I dreamed you a pot of gold

like the sun on a shoestring
of rainbow, the last thread not violet
but lavender, its frequency vibrato

like spring in bed, yes! You were
a ribbon of colour tied to the balloon
of my heart. But soon familiarity

set in, conspired with secrets to keep
knowledge at the slice of open door.
Every day I felt a change to the way

my eyes spooled you in. We realigned.
You lost your tether, snapped lavender,
and my balloon lifted away again.

THE WAYS I MIGHT LOVE YOU, GIVEN THE CHANCE

1.
I might cuddle you on cold mornings,
both of us in flannel dressing gowns,
sipping mugs of Irish hot chocolate
with a cat sliding between our limbs.

2.
I might be so shocked at your touch,
electrified to a fossil,
that I merely stand, an adoring statue
while the fridge door hangs open.

3.
I might bed you in reams of poetry
dedicated to your eyes, your lips,
your toenails, your verrucas,
while you gradually suffocate.

4.
I might cook your dinner
and never work again,
as you go out and bring home
the Quorn meat-free bacon.

5.
I might brandish a whip,
chain you to the bed,
and make Sadeian demands
you can never meet.

6.
But I might just be me
loving you,
with the bills and the shopping
and sod-all on TV.

FRUIT

You call me a fruit,
and I agree,
say

a fruit is ripe,
promising seeds,
bursting with juice.

You call me a fruit,
as though a vegetable
while I recite a litany
of fresh attributes:

a fruit is rich,
remembers its roots,
nourishes, quenches,
makes a display of any table.

I say,
I am the apple
that announces the gravity
of a given situation;
I am the pomegranate
whose gemstones teach
of the burden of possession;
I am the fig
our ancestors couldn't resist.

You call me a fruit
and I agree:
soft, round and sweet.
Peel back my layers,
take a look at my pips.
Full as a melon,
sharp as a lime,
come over here
and bite me.